TOUGH
LIFE
LESSONS

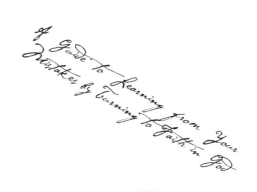

A Guide to Learning from Your Mistakes by Turning to Faith in God

ANDREW KALITKA

WINEPRESS WP PUBLISHING

ISBN 1-57921-799-0
Library of Congress Catalog Card Number: 2005904589

Table of Contents

SECTION TWO: STORIES OF FAITH

Introduction

Most people do not understand Jesus. Only some people can. And even those who can understand Jesus often don't. Jesus spoke about a spiritual kingdom, and He spoke in parables. Read this parable about someone planting seeds, spoken by Jesus in Mark 4:3-9. Does it tell you anything?

> Listen! Behold, a sower went out to sow. And it happened, as he sowed, that some seed fell by the wayside; and the birds of the air came and devoured it. Some fell on stony ground, where it did not have much earth; and immediately it sprang up because it had no depth of earth. But when the sun was up it was scorched, and because it had no root it withered away. And some seed fell among thorns; and the thorns grew up and choked it, and it

yielded no crop. But other seed fell on good ground and yielded a crop that sprang up, increased and produced: some thirtyfold, some sixty, and some a hundred. . . . He who has ears to hear, let him hear!

Did you find this parable hard to understand? If so, you are not alone. Jesus even had to explain this parable to His closest followers. One would think that Jesus spoke in parables to make Himself clear to all His hearers. But actually, it was so He would be understood only by those to whom it has been given to know "the mysteries of the kingdom of heaven" (Matt. 13:11).

Here is how Jesus explained this parable to His closest followers (Matt. 13:19-23):

When anyone hears the word of the kingdom, and does not understand it, then the wicked one comes and snatches away what was sown in his heart. This is he who received seed by the wayside. But he who received the seed on stony places, this is he who hears the word and immediately receives it with joy; yet he has no root in himself, but endures only for a while. For when tribulation or persecution arises because of the word, immediately he stumbles.

Now he who received seed among the thorns is he who hears the word, and the cares of this world and the deceitfulness of riches choke the word, and he becomes unfruitful. But he who received seed on the good ground is he who hears the word and understands it, who indeed bears fruit and produces: some a hundredfold, some sixty, some thirty.

"HOW DO I CHANGE MY SOIL?"

After hearing me read this parable, a young woman in Africa asked this question: "How do I change my soil?" She was ready to enter the kingdom of heaven. Everyone who enters the kingdom of heaven enters the same way, by believing the following concept and making it an honest prayer to God:

> I am a sinner whose sin has separated me from my Creator. Only God's grace through the sacrifice of His sinless one and only Son Jesus Christ can redeem me to the relationship with God that I desire. I believe that my good works are powerless to get me into heaven. Only God's sacrifice of His Son can give me entrance into heaven, and I receive this gift that God has freely given me. Amen.

Many of you prayed this prayer long ago, and some of you are considering saying this prayer now. Feel free to turn back to this introduction at any time. If you have just said this prayer, I am overjoyed! God's free gift will change your life!

My goal in writing this book is to reveal various "Obstacles to Faith" that cause our soil to seem stony, thorny, or poor like the wayside. Following, you will find many "Stories of Faith" that clarify what good soil is like. I hope you find this book insightful and meaningful.

Andrew Kalitka
Gloucester, Massachusetts

SECTION ONE:
OBSTACLES TO FAITH

1 Postmodernism and Moral Relativism

In our 21st century world, we are in the middle of a cultural worldview shift that has slowly crept upon us and overtaken many of us. Even Bible-believing Christians have let the ideas of postmodernism saturate their vocabularies and their thoughts. Basically, Western societies as a whole no longer accept that we have moral absolutes that come from a Moral Lawgiver. For example, the news media tend to refer to those who defend posting the Ten Commandments in public squares as "emotional" debaters.

Up until less than a hundred years ago, those who defended posting the Ten Commandments in public would have been classified as intellectual debaters. Do you see the shift? Intellectual debates lead to rational conclusions, but emotional debates lead to dead end discussions. Those who defend posting the Ten Commandments are now marginalized as being less level-headed and more given towards emotional outbursts.

Why is this significant? Because it implicitly discredits the Bible itself. It implies that the Bible is OK as long as it is not taken too seriously, and it makes our own subjective perception of reality more important than anything God Himself revealed in the Bible.

QUESTIONS FOR
DISCUSSION OR REFLECTION

- Is your faith in God a postmodern, self-centered faith?

  _____

  _____

  _____

- Or is your faith in God a Bible-based, God-centered faith?

  _____

  _____

  _____

2 The Mind of the Sadducees

—Matthew 22:23-33

T he Sadducees were a group of people who presupposed that God's spiritual power in the world and in the Bible could not be taken seriously. They did not believe in the resurrection. With their own firmly held presuppositions in mind, the Sadducees asked Jesus a detailed question about an imagined scenario that could cause a complication in heaven after a resurrection. The Sadducees thought they were giving Jesus a reality check, as though the Sadducees were the mature authority and Jesus needed to be taught a lesson. But Jesus' answer silenced the Sadducees and astonished the crowd around them. Jesus told them they were mistaken, or had deceived themselves with their own question. He successfully answered their specific question about the resurrection and then added, "But concerning the resurrection of the dead, have you not read what was spoken to you by God, saying, 'I am the God of Abraham, the God of Isaac, and the God of Jacob'? God is not the God of the dead, but of the living" (Matt. 22:31-32).

Do you understand what Jesus said? When the Bible calls God the God of Abraham, Isaac, and Jacob, the Bible means that these are living, resurrected men in heaven. We can develop the same false ideas the Sadducees had, discounting the resurrection and other seemingly foreign spiritual ideas. And we can develop self-confidence in our own mistaken understanding of the world.

QUESTIONS FOR
DISCUSSION OR REFLECTION

- Do you really believe in the resurrection?

  _____

  _____

  _____

- If you do not really believe in the resurrection, are you willing to consider that you are
  deceiving yourself? Why or why not?

  _____

  _____

  _____

The Mind of the Pharisees

—Matthew 23:1-36

The Pharisees were the authorities who taught the law of Moses to the Jewish people. They were identified as hypocrites by Jesus, because they made the burden of keeping the law harder than it had to be, and yet they were not following their own laws, which were more stringent than the original law of Moses.

The key to understanding why Jesus was so concerned about the influence of the Pharisees is found in Matthew 23:13. "But woe to you, scribes and Pharisees, hypocrites! For you shut up the kingdom of heaven against men; for you neither go in yourselves, nor do you allow those who are entering to go in." The Pharisees, by making people focus on outward appearance and superficial conformity to rules, were keeping entire assemblies away from the kingdom of heaven. The kingdom of heaven is spiritual, and any attempt to do good works for the sake of obeying rules or meeting expectations is an attempt to live apart from the spiritual realm.

QUESTIONS FOR
DISCUSSION OR REFLECTION

- Who in your life is keeping your mind focused on earthly works, rather than on the spiritual kingdom you belong to as a Christian?

  _____

  _____

  _____

- If nobody else is, are you doing it to yourself?

  _____

  _____

  _____

- Are you doing it to other people?

  _____

  _____

  _____

4 Repeating the Original Sin of Adam and Eve

—Genesis 2:15-17; Genesis 3:1-6

W e repeat the original sin of Adam and Eve by acting on the idea that total freedom could be more rewarding than obedience to God's commands. God gave Adam just one restriction in the garden of Eden: "Of every tree of the garden you may freely eat; but of the tree of the knowledge of good and evil you shall not eat, for in the day that you eat of it you shall surely die" (Gen. 2:16-17). But notice how subtly the serpent twisted God's words when he tempted Eve: "You will not surely die. For God knows that in the day you eat of it your eyes will be opened, and you will be like God, knowing good and evil" (Gen. 3:4-5).

The serpent's deception would have fooled you, too, wouldn't it? It would have fooled me. When Adam and Eve fell for that temptation and ate that fruit, they were committing the Original Sin, giving the human race the sin nature that we all have. We all fall for the temptation that total freedom could be more rewarding than obedience to God's commands. It is our earliest struggle as young children, and it is our most common struggle as adults. It is called sin.

QUESTIONS FOR
DISCUSSION OR REFLECTION

■ Has this lesson changed your perspective of your own sin nature? If so, how?

_____

_____

_____

■ Do you agree that it is a deception that "total freedom could be more rewarding than obedience to God's commands"?

_____

_____

_____

■ Do you know enough about God's commands to know when you are being tempted to break them?

_____

_____

_____

Repeating the Error of Balaam

—Numbers 22-25; Numbers 31:16;
2 Peter 2:15; Jude 11; Revelation 2:14

By corrupting people who cannot be cursed, we repeat the error of Balaam, an Old Testament prophet who was very close to God. Everyone Balaam blessed was blessed. Everyone Balaam cursed was cursed. He prophesied only what God wanted him to say. Balaam also put himself up for hire, allowing people to pay him to travel and prophesy.

A dilemma occurred when an enemy of Israel offered to pay Balaam substantially to curse Israel. Knowing that God would not curse Israel, Balaam compromised and went anyway, agreeing to tell them only what God would show him. So God gave Balaam the words to say, and it was a blessing of Israel. Israel's enemy then moved Balaam to another location so he could curse Israel from there. But the words God gave Balaam were an even more beautiful blessing of

Israel than the first blessing. And yet again, a third time Balaam blessed Israel from still another location. He then prophesied the demise of the enemies he was speaking to.

Shortly after this, the men of Israel began to marry the foreign women through the counsel of Balaam (Num. 31:16). This harlotry culminated with Israelites sacrificing to false gods at the urging of the foreign women. It angered God and led to a plague that killed 24,000 in Israel. This corruption of Israel was caused by Balaam's willingness to pursue earthly gain at the expense of the purity of those whom God would not curse. Israel's purity was corrupted.

QUESTIONS FOR DISCUSSION OR REFLECTION

■ Is there corruption in your life that has resulted from pursuit of earthly gain?

_____

_____

_____

■ Are you aware that your purity should not be corrupted in the pursuit of reaching non-Christians for Christ?

_____

_____

_____

■ If you are a pastor, are you aware that you should not corrupt your congregation in order to attract non-Christians to your church?

_____

_____

_____

Bad Shepherds

—Ezekiel 34; Acts 20:28-30;
2 Peter 2:15-22; Revelation 2:14-17

W hen you read the word "shepherd," think "pastor." They come from the same Greek word in the original Greek New Testament. Bad shepherds are characterized by feeding themselves with their sheep. These shepherds feed their own sinful, fleshly desires by preaching clever, lofty words that sound righteous but actually appeal to the congregation's fleshly lusts. "While they promise them liberty, they themselves are slaves to corruption" (2 Pet. 2:19). Ruling with force and cruelty, they cause their sheep to scatter, without searching for them (Ezek. 34:4-6). They even move beyond corrupting themselves and their congregations, and preach corruption to their congregations as a righteous sounding doctrine (Rev. 2:14-15).

If you belong to a congregation that unfortunately resembles what was just described, you have hope. God will rescue you and feed you Himself as your Good Shepherd. Ezekiel 34:12 says, "As a shepherd seeks out his flock on the day he is among his scattered sheep, so I will seek out My sheep and deliver them from all the places where they were scattered on a cloudy and dark day." Furthermore, Revelation 2:17 says, "To him who overcomes I will give some of the hidden manna to eat. And I will give him a white stone, and on the stone a new name written which no one knows except him who receives it." If you are a true believer with a bad shepherd, God will feed you Himself! In fact, even if your pastor is a good shepherd, Jesus Christ is the Good Shepherd of you and your pastor alike (Ps. 23; Jn. 10:11-16).

QUESTIONS FOR
DISCUSSION OR REFLECTION

■ Does your pastor feed you spiritually like a good shepherd, or does he cleverly appeal to your flesh?

_____

_____

_____

■ Does your pastor rule with force and cruelty, or with gentleness?

_____

_____

_____

■ If you have a bad shepherd, are you willing to "scatter," letting God feed you, while you find a church with a good shepherd?

_____

_____

_____

Compromising Your Faith in Order to Pursue a Spouse

—1 Kings 11; Numbers 25;
Judges 16; 2 Corinthians 6:14

These days, broken relationships and broken families are the rule, not the exception. Whether it be by divorce, separation, death, abuse, or dysfunction, many of us have suffered deep wounds from a young age in our own families. Then when it comes to finding a spouse as an adult, the pursuit seems like a fruitless ordeal. Well meaning, devout Christians sometimes can't even decipher the loving intents of other well meaning, devout Christians. Singles can be so bad at expressing interest in one another that pursuing a spouse can become the most difficult trial in a Christian's life. The problem is compounded with the realization that there is no easy solution. There is rarely a shortcut to marriage, and there is rarely total conviction that one is supposed to stay single permanently.

Devoted Christians have a definite priority regarding whom to marry. It can be summed up in this statement: do not marry someone who will distract from your devotion to God. This rules out non-Christians (2 Cor. 6:14). The Bible contains numerous examples of devastating consequences when people who believe in the one true God marry outside their faith. It leads to compromising with the faith of the non-Christian spouse, which turns the Christian's heart away from God. Examples include Solomon in 1 Kings 11, and the Israelites at the time of Balaam (Num. 25). Also, do not fall for the temptations of those you do not marry. They, too, will turn your heart from God. This happened to Samson in Judges 16.

QUESTIONS FOR
DISCUSSION OR REFLECTION

■ Is your search for a spouse a difficult ordeal?
Explain.

_____

_____

_____

■ Are you willing to keep your devotion to God
your top priority?

_____

_____

_____

Mature Sinfulness

—1 Corinthians 14:20; Galatians 5:16-26;
John 15:1-5; Mark 7:20-23

The Bible commands Christians to be mature in understanding but like infants regarding sinfulness (1 Cor. 14:20). In other words, we are to have depth of understanding regarding godly characteristics. Yet we are to have undeveloped sinful characteristics. We are not supposed to be mature sinners! As Christians, we either walk in the flesh or in the Spirit. The flesh and the Spirit are opposed to each other (Gal. 5:16-26):

> Now the works of the flesh are evident, which are: adultery, fornication, uncleanness, lewdness, idolatry, sorcery, hatred, contentions, jealousies, outbursts of wrath, selfish ambitions, dissensions, heresies, envy, murders, drunkenness, revelries, and the like. . . . But

the fruit of the Spirit is love, joy, peace, longsuffering, kindness, goodness, faithfulness, gentleness, self-control. Against such there is no law. And those who are Christ's have crucified the flesh with its passions and desires. If we live in the Spirit, let us also walk in the Spirit. Let us not become conceited, provoking one another, envying one another.

QUESTIONS FOR DISCUSSION OR REFLECTION

- Examine your heart. What are you living for? What motivates you?

  _____

  _____

  _____

- If you were to tell the most fascinating stories in your life, which list describes your stories better? Is it the "works of the flesh," or the "fruit of the Spirit?"

  _____

  _____

  _____

- Which list do you understand better? Are you a mature sinner?

  _____

  _____

  _____

- How deep is your understanding of the fruit of the Spirit?

  _____

  _____

  _____

SECTION TWO:
STORIES OF FAITH

9 Creation

—Hebrews 11:3, Romans 8:18-25,
John 1:1-3,14; Genesis 1-2

B y faith we understand that the worlds were framed by the word of God, so that the things which are seen were not made of things which are visible" (Heb. 11:3). Hebrews 11 reminds us of the faith of many men and women from Old Testament times, and it encourages Christians to live by similar faith. Most of the people mentioned in the "Stories of Faith" section of this book are also mentioned in Hebrews 11. Some are not.

It is noteworthy that before mentioning specific examples of people expressing faith, nature itself is mentioned. Faith in God is an all encompassing faith. This is faith in an invisible all powerful God, not just faith in invisible things. "The word of God" mentioned in Hebrews 11:3 is reminiscent of John 1:1-3, 14:

In the beginning was the Word, and the Word was with God, and the Word was God. He was in the beginning with God. All things were made through Him, and without Him nothing was made that was made. . . . And the Word became flesh and dwelt among us, and we beheld His glory, the glory as of the only begotten of the Father, full of grace and truth.

Jesus Christ is the Word that John is describing in these verses. Jesus was there in the beginning, with the Father and the Holy Spirit, as one God, creating the universe. The same God who spoke all of nature into existence (Gen. 1-2) came to redeem it from its fallen condition.

It is not only people who are hindered in this fallen world. All of creation groans in eager expectation for the redemption of the human race and nature with it. Christians also groan within, because even though the Holy Spirit indwells us, our bodies need redemption so that our hope for glory can become reality (Rom. 8:19-23). "But if we hope for what we do not see, we eagerly wait for it with perseverance" (Rom. 8:25).

QUESTIONS FOR
DISCUSSION OR REFLECTION

- How deeply does your spirit groan for your sin-prone, weary body's redemption?

  _____

  _____

  _____

- Do you want your body to be redeemed? (In other words, do you want the new body you will receive after your resurrection?)

  _____

  _____

  _____

- Do you consider your sinful desires to be a hindrance to your spirit's deepest longings? Or are you satisfied with submitting to your body's weaknesses?

  _____

  _____

  _____

- Does creation groan for redemption more than you do?

  _____

  _____

  _____

10 Job: An Innocent Man in Agony

The book of Job is about a man named Job who was "blameless and upright, and one who feared God and shunned evil" (Job 1:1). Job was an astonishingly good man. Then tragedy struck. He lost his children and his many possessions all in one day. Not even this would cause him to sin. Then his skin became covered with painful boils on his entire body. And still, Job did not sin. His wife told him, "Do you still hold fast to your integrity? Curse God and die!" But he said to her, "You speak as one of the foolish women speaks. Shall we indeed accept good from God, and shall we not accept adversity?" (Job 2:9-10).

Three friends come from distant towns to comfort Job. They listen as Job laments, wishing he had never been born. Job and his friends talk things through quite thoroughly. His friends continually guess how Job could have brought the miseries upon himself. Job speaks of his pain, which multiplies with his need to defend himself to his friends. Then, in chapter 38, the Lord speaks to Job out of a whirlwind. God asks Job a long series of questions built around His rule over all creation. God's first question is, "Where were you when I laid the foundations of the earth?" (Job 38:4). And after God's series of detailed questions about nature, God asks Job,

> Shall the one who contends
> with the Almighty correct Him?
> He who rebukes God, let him answer it.

Then Job answered the Lord and said:

> Behold, I am vile;
> What shall I answer you?
> I lay my hand over my mouth.
> Once I have spoken, but I will not answer;
> Yes, twice, but I will proceed no further
>
> —Job 40:2-6

Job came to realize that there was no need to consider how good a man he was. As a man, he was basically sinful and dependent on God's mercy. In Job 42:5-6, Job tells the Lord,

I have heard of You by the hearing of the ear,
But now my eye sees You.
Therefore I abhor myself,
And repent in dust and ashes.

Then the Lord expresses anger at Job's three friends for representing God falsely in their foolish advise. And after Job prays for his friends, God blesses Job again (Job 42:10). Job's possessions become double what they were before the tragedies, and he has the same number of children again. He also lives many more years, enjoying life with his children and grandchildren.

When Job was in the middle of his deepest pain, multiplied by his friends' unwise counsel, he said a few words that hinted at a coming "mediator" and "Redeemer," Jesus Christ. In Job 9:32-33 and 19:25, Job says of God,

For He is not a man, as I am,
That I may answer Him,
And that we should go to court together.
Nor is there any mediator between us,
Who may lay his hand on us both.

For I know that my Redeemer lives,
And He shall stand at last on the earth.

In Job's lowest moments of hopelessness, he felt an acute longing for the coming of God's Son, Jesus Christ, whose coming was still in the distant future.

QUESTIONS FOR
DISCUSSION OR REFLECTION

■ How righteous does God think you are?

_____

_____

_____

■ If God thinks you are extraordinarily righteous, what would hurt more: tragedy and loss, or friends who multiply your pain by guessing how you might have brought the pain on yourself?

_____

_____

_____

■ Are you willing to forgive friends who multiply your pain?

_____

_____

_____

11 Elijah and John the Baptist

—1 Kings 18:17-40; Matthew 3:1-17, 11:14;
Luke 1:17; Malachi 4:5-6

In 1 Kings 18, the prophet Elijah issued a challenge to 450 prophets of false gods. The prophets accepted the challenge. These 450 false prophets prepared a sacrifice to be burned, except they did not start the fire. Instead, they called out to their gods to send fire. But nothing happened. None of the gods sent fire, regardless of how much the prophets pleaded. Then Elijah took the same challenge, and added a major degree of difficulty.

Elijah stepped up, prepared a sacrifice to God, and then drenched the sacrifice and the trench around it with a large amount of water. Then he called out to God. 1 Kings 18:38-39 tells what happened next: "Then the fire of the LORD fell and consumed the burnt sacrifice, and the wood and the stones and the dust, and it licked up the water that was in the trench. Now when all the people saw it, they fell on their faces; and they said, 'The LORD, He is God! The LORD, He is God!'"

Centuries later, John the Baptist came to prepare the way for Jesus' ministry. John lived in the wilderness, wore camel's hair, and ate locusts and wild honey. He preached, "Repent, for the kingdom of heaven is at hand!" (Matt. 3:2), and "I indeed baptize you with water unto repentance, but He who is coming after me is mightier than I, whose sandals I am not worthy to carry. He will baptize you with the Holy Spirit and fire" (Matt. 3:11).

The similarity between Elijah and John the Baptist is deeper than just "water and fire." It is about God choosing unlikely means to prepare for His wonders. God does not need our help. He wants us to realize our helplessness and the futility of our attempts at self-sufficiency. Jesus' first words in the Sermon on the Mount (Matt. 5:3) were: "Blessed are the poor in spirit, For theirs is the kingdom of heaven."

"Poor in spirit" means awareness that we are spiritually helpless apart from God. It is the opposite of self-sufficient pride. It is also different than developing strong family ties, friendships, and communities. Focusing on these earthly relationships invariably leads to compromise. When either these relationships or self-sufficiency are given top priority, sin eventually arises. And sin leads to cover-ups, pride, boasting, stubbornness, and more sin. However, when we remember our spiritual helplessness apart from God, we repent, confess our sins, and receive God's forgiveness.

QUESTIONS FOR
DISCUSSION OR REFLECTION

■ How self-sufficient are you? Do you really think you need God in your life?

_____

_____

_____

■ Do you let earthly relationships overtake your relationship with God as your top priority?

_____

_____

_____

■ Do you keep in mind that God does not need our help before He can do great things, or are you tempted by strategies to "help God out" by making repentance seem less invasive than it really is?

_____

_____

_____

The Scribe Who Was 12 "Not Far from the Kingdom of God"

—Mark 12:28-34

Scribes were close companions to Pharisees. They performed different roles, but both based their beliefs on close scrutiny of the Old Testament laws. Scribes and Pharisees presumed that Jesus simply scrutinized the laws differently. Therefore, they misinterpreted Jesus' words and intentions and tried to disprove Jesus' scrutiny of the laws.

One scribe, however, was open-minded enough to ask Jesus a more revealing question. He asked, "Which is the first commandment of all?" The scribe was investigating whether or not Jesus had an unwise bias, not just assuming Jesus had an unwise bias. The rest of the conversation, recorded in Mark 12:29-34, speaks for itself:

Jesus answered him, "The first of all the commandments is: 'Hear, O Israel, the LORD our God, the LORD is one. And you shall love the LORD your God with all your heart, with all your soul, with all your mind, and with all your strength.' This is the first commandment. And the second, like it, is this: 'You shall love your neighbor as yourself.' There is no other commandment greater than these." So the scribe said to Him, "Well said, Teacher. You have spoken the truth, for there is one God, and there is no other but He. And to love Him with all the heart, with all the understanding, with all the soul, and with all the strength, and to love one's neighbor as oneself, is more than all the whole burnt offerings and sacrifices." Now when Jesus saw that he answered wisely, He said to him, "You are not far from the kingdom of God."

QUESTIONS FOR
DISCUSSION OR REFLECTION

■ Do you often find yourself bogged down by worries about less important commandments, and forget about the two most important ones?

_____

_____

_____

■ What do you think motivated this scribe to speak up in agreement with Jesus?

_____

_____

_____

■ Is it easy to obey these two greatest commandments? Why or why not?

_____

_____

_____

13 Abel

—Genesis 4:1-10, Hebrews 11:4

By faith Abel offered to God a more excellent sacrifice than Cain, through which he obtained witness that he was righteous, God testifying of his gifts; and through it he being dead still speaks" (Heb. 11:4). Cain and Abel were sons of Adam and Eve. Both sons offered sacrifices to God. God respected Abel's sacrifice, because Abel sacrificed his first and best. But God did not respect Cain's sacrifice, because Cain sacrificed ordinary things instead of his first and best.

Cain became very angry, and God tried to counsel him. If Cain had reconsidered and offered God his best sacrifice, God would have accepted it. But instead, Cain let his anger control him. Cain murdered Abel in a field.

Abel's proper view of God resulted in his appropriate sacrifice to God. Everything Abel had, and even his life, was ultimately God's. So the appropriate sacrifice to God was his first and best, not just of his possessions, but the first and best of his heart, soul, and strength. If your view of God is right, then it will easily follow that you will give God your first and best.

Cain had more of a "one for You, one for me" view of sacrificing to God. This view may not seem horrible at first glance. But upon closer analysis, this view requires that you either reduce God to your level or raise yourself to God's level. And then, it is only a matter of time before anger or other sinful attitudes control you and result in terrible consequences.

QUESTIONS FOR
DISCUSSION OR REFLECTION

■ Do you have a heart like Abel's, willing to give God your first and best?

_____

_____

_____

■ If you have a heart like Abel's, are you often hindered by people who resemble Cain and form opposition to you?

_____

_____

_____

■ Are you like Cain, believing that you are in good standing with God, when really you have lowered Him to your level?

_____

_____

_____

■ If so, will you change your perspective before it causes you to thwart the efforts of the Abels in your life?

_____

_____

_____

14 Enoch

—Genesis 5:22-24; Hebrews 11:5-6

B_y faith Enoch was taken away so that he did not see death, 'and was not found, because God had taken him'; for before he was taken he had this testimony, that he pleased God. But without faith it is impossible to please Him, for he who comes to God must believe that He is, and that He is a rewarder of those who diligently seek Him" (Heb. 11:5-6).

The Bible does not tell us much about Enoch. There is no story about any major accomplishments or fame. We just know that he walked with God all his life after becoming a father, and then "he was not, for God took him" (Gen. 5:24). He did not die. Enoch diligently sought God, and God rewarded Enoch by taking him away.

QUESTIONS FOR
DISCUSSION OR REFLECTION

■ What do you think about God rewarding Enoch by taking him straight from life on earth into God's direct presence?

_____

_____

_____

■ Imagine God calling you into His direct presence right now. Does this sound like a reward, or a threat?

_____

_____

_____

■ How strong is your faith in God? How diligently do you seek Him?

_____

_____

_____

15 Noah

—Genesis 6-9; Hebrews 11:7

By faith Noah, being divinely warned of things not yet seen, moved with godly fear, prepared an ark for the saving of his household, by which he condemned the world and became heir of the righteousness which is according to faith" (Heb. 11:7). Noah, like Enoch, "walked with God" (Gen. 6:9). God asked Noah, who had neither seen rain nor lived near a large body of water, to build an ark. Looking quite foolish, he built a giant boat according to the exact specifications God gave him. Noah also built with the understanding that God would condemn the world with the Flood, destroying all who were not protected in the ark (Gen. 6:13).

This Flood would change the earth's atmosphere permanently. It dramatically limited the years people lived.

Before the Flood, people lived about 900 years, according to the genealogies of Genesis 5. But after the Flood, people's life spans soon dipped to 120 years and younger. The Flood took place with Noah, his sons, his wife, and his sons' wives surviving in the ark along with animals. And the whole world was destroyed. There was a new start for humanity in a very different world after the waters finally subsided.

What can we learn about faith from Noah? The key is in Hebrews 11:7. Noah accepted the fact that God decided to condemn most of the world. And he accepted the fact that he was among the few God decided to rescue. By trusting God and obeying His commands, Noah prepared for a future event that his mind could not fathom.

Most people will choose to reject God and suffer His condemnation. This is one of the most difficult truths of the Bible. Even Jesus affirmed this, saying that many go the way that leads to destruction, but few find the narrow, difficult way that leads to life (Matt. 7:13-14). A frequently asked question is, "How can an all powerful, all loving God create people only to condemn and destroy them?" This is a legitimate question. God seems like a bully. But this is why Jesus Christ is so important. The Son of God Himself, our Creator, came to earth as a Man and suffered cruelly in order to save some. Without Jesus, God still seems like the Almighty Bully. With Jesus, God is the Almighty Hero. Is a bully still a bully after he suffers and dies while saving some of his victims? Of course not. In fact, it makes one reconsider whether he was truly a bully at all.

Noah "became an heir of the righteousness that is according to faith" (Heb. 11:7). Noah trusted God even when God seemed cruel, believing that God was completely good and trustworthy. Thousands of years before Jesus lived, Noah was His heir. This is because Jesus is the Creator. Jesus' righteousness is from eternity past, not just from 2,000 years ago. Jesus' death and resurrection was for those who believed in Him after His time, and for those who believed in Him before it. Believers before His time did not know that He would be called "Jesus," but they trusted in God's righteousness and became heirs to it.

QUESTIONS FOR DISCUSSION OR REFLECTION

- Like Noah, we believers have received promises from God that we will be among the few rescued while most of the world is condemned and destroyed. Does this make you skeptical of God's goodness?

  _____

  _____

  _____

- Like Noah, we are commanded to prepare for a future in a different world that we cannot accurately imagine. We are to prepare our souls for our eternal home. How much time do you waste trying to make your soul feel at home in this world?

  _____

  _____

  _____

- How much time do you spend reading the Bible and pursuing spiritual understanding of God's goodness and righteousness?

  _____

  _____

  _____

16 Abraham

—Genesis 12-15; Hebrews 11:8-10;
John 14:1-6

By faith Abraham obeyed when he was called to go out to the place which he would receive as an inheritance. And he went out, not knowing where he was going. By faith he dwelt in the land of promise as in a foreign country, dwelling in tents with Isaac and Jacob, the heirs with him of the same promise; for he waited for the city which has foundations, whose builder and maker is God" (Heb. 11:8-10).

Abraham was seventy-five years old when he obeyed God's command in Genesis 12:1-3:

> Get out of your country,
> From your family
> And from your father's house,
> To a land that I will show you.

71

I will make you a great nation;
I will bless you
And make your name great;
And you shall be a blessing.
I will bless those who bless you,
And I will curse him who curses you;
And in you all the families of the earth shall be blessed.

Abraham and his wife Sarah were elderly and childless, and Sarah was barren. Yet Abraham believed God's promises. God told Abraham that, contrary to what he would naturally think, he would be the physical father of his heirs. Then God brought Abraham outside and said, "Look now toward heaven, and count the stars if you are able to number them. . . . So shall your descendants be" (Gen. 15:5). The next verse says, "And he believed in the LORD, and He accounted it to him for righteousness."

How could Abraham have such faith? He must have trusted that God could do the impossible. Furthermore, as Hebrews 11:10 says, Abraham "waited for the city which has foundations, whose builder and maker is God." This is the heavenly city, New Jerusalem. There wasn't even a Jerusalem on earth yet, and Abraham's faith hinged on his hope for the heavenly one. This is hinted at in Genesis 12:3, "And in you all the families of the earth shall be blessed." Not just Abraham and his heirs, but every family on earth would be blessed through Abraham. Jesus was Abraham's heir (Matt. 1:1), and Jesus is the One preparing "the city which has foundations." In John 14:1-3, Jesus said, "Let not your heart be troubled; you believe in God, believe also in Me. In My Father's house are many mansions; if it were not so, I would have told you. And if I go and prepare a place for you, I will come back again and receive you to Myself; that where I am, there you may be also."

QUESTIONS FOR
DISCUSSION OR REFLECTION

■   Do you make absurd looking steps of faith in
    your life? If so, do you make sure that your
    hope is placed in your heavenly home?

    _____

    _____

    _____

■   Are your deepest longings based on what you
    want in this life, or what you wish for based
    on God's promises for eternal life?

    _____

    _____

    _____

17 Sarah

—Genesis 16-21; Hebrews 11:11-16

By faith Sarah herself also received strength to conceive seed, and she bore a child when she was past the age, because she judged Him faithful who had promised. Therefore from one man, and him as good as dead, were born as many as the stars of the sky in multitude—innumerable as the sand which is by the seashore. These all died in faith, not having received the promises, but having seen them afar off were assured of them, embraced them and confessed that they were strangers and pilgrims on the earth. For those who say such things declare plainly that they seek a homeland. And truly if they had called to mind that country from which they had come out, they would have had opportunity to return. But now they desire a better, that is, a heavenly country. Therefore God is not ashamed to be called their God, for He has prepared a city for them" (Heb. 11:11-16).

Both Abraham and Sarah had lapses of faith when times got difficult. Sarah asked Abraham to conceive a child through Sarah's servant Hagar (Gen. 16). And Abraham intentionally misled authorities twice, telling them that Sarah was his sister (Gen. 12:10-20; Gen. 20). But when it came to trusting God at His word, both Abraham and Sarah were faithful.

In this case (Gen. 18:9-15), Sarah laughed when she overheard God telling Abraham that she would conceive a child through her husband when she was 90 years old and he was 100. Sarah was not laughing out of scorn or disbelief. She and Abraham both believed. But it was funny!

God was true to His promise, and Abraham's son Isaac was born (Gen. 21:1-8). The name Isaac means "laughter." In Genesis 21:6, Sarah said, "God has made me laugh, and all who hear will laugh with me."

QUESTIONS FOR
DISCUSSION OR REFLECTION

- Can you think of examples from your life in which God provided for you in funny ways?

  _____

  _____

  _____

- Was your faith a contributing factor in God's blessings? (If you don't think so, think again.)

  _____

  _____

  _____

18 Abraham

—Genesis 22:1-18; Hebrews 11:17-19

B y faith Abraham, when he was tested, offered up Isaac, and he who had received the promises offered up his only begotten son, of whom it was said, 'In Isaac your seed shall be called,' concluding that God was able to raise him up, even from the dead, from which he also received him in a figurative sense" (Heb. 11:17-19).

Let's review Abraham's story. When Abraham was 75 years old, God told him to leave his home and travel to a place where he would become a great nation. His son Isaac was born when Abraham was 100. And then, when Isaac became a young man, God asked Abraham to kill Isaac as a burnt offering (Gen. 22:1-2). And Abraham obeyed! The Angel of the LORD called out to stop him, and Abraham stopped (Gen. 22:11-13). He sacrificed a ram instead.

This was an ultimate test of where Abraham placed his faith. He believed in an all powerful God who is faithful to His word, and who could resurrect the dead. Notice that Abraham had to travel three days to get to the place where he was to sacrifice his son (Gen. 22:4). Just as Abraham had to endure three days of uncertainty and despair before receiving Isaac from the dead figuratively, followers of Jesus had to endure three days of uncertainty and despair before they received Jesus from the dead literally.

QUESTIONS FOR
DISCUSSION OR REFLECTION

- Do you believe that God is faithful to His promise to resurrect you to eternal life?

  _____

  _____

  _____

- Are you willing to base your most important decisions in life on God's eternal promises rather than on what seems safe or right for the time being?

  _____

  _____

  _____

19 Isaac

—Genesis 27; Hebrews 11:20

B y faith Isaac blessed Jacob and Esau concerning things to come" (Heb. 11:20). Before Isaac and Rebekah's twin sons were born, God told Rebekah:

> Two nations are in your womb,
> Two peoples shall be separated from your body;
> One people shall be stronger than the other,
> And the older shall serve the younger.
>
> —Gen. 25:23

Esau was born first, and in two instances that seemed tragic for Esau, Jacob took his older brother's birthright and blessing (Gen. 25:27-34; Gen. 27:1-40). As an old man with poor eyesight, Isaac presented his blessing to Jacob, thinking he was giving it to Esau (Gen. 27:27-29). Normally, that would be the end of it. Just one blessing. But instead, Isaac gave a lesser, but still significant, blessing to Esau as well (Gen. 27:39-40). It is for this that Isaac is honored in Hebrews 11:20.

Isaac's act of faith in blessing both sons is similar to the role Jesus played in extending God's blessing of grace to gentiles as well as Jews. Without Jesus, God's eternal blessings would only be readily accessible to Jewish people. With Jesus, God's eternal blessings are readily accessible to every people group on earth. Isaac believed in a God who would extend His blessing to every people group all around the world, and God honored that faith.

QUESTIONS FOR
DISCUSSION OR REFLECTION

■ Do you lose hope in God's eternal blessings when you see God bless others more than you in this life? Do you ever lose sight of eternity completely?

_____

_____

_____

■ How does Jesus' role in history affect your view of God's willingness to bless you and love you?

_____

_____

_____

20 Jacob

—Genesis 47:27-49:33; Hebrews 11:21

B y faith Jacob, when he was dying, blessed each of the sons of Joseph, and worshiped, leaning on the top of his staff" (Heb. 11:21). Jacob lived a difficult, complicated life. He labored hard for 14 years to obtain two wives, only one of which he loved (Gen. 29). His home life was filled with envy, sorrow, and competition (Gen. 30-35). He lived many years in sorrow over the loss of his beloved, favorite son Joseph (Gen. 37:31-35). He later learned that Joseph had not died after all (Gen. 45:25-28). And in his old age, he endured drought and famine (Gen. 42-45). His final seventeen years were spent in Egypt, where he experienced prosperity (Gen. 47).

When Jacob's death was imminent, he blessed Joseph's two young sons. Like his father Isaac, Jacob blessed the younger brother with a greater blessing than the older brother (Gen. 48:11-22). But Jacob did this knowingly, not by mistake. In his blessing, he said that the younger brother's "descendants shall be a multitude of nations" (Gen. 48:19). It is for this blessing that Jacob's faith is honored in Hebrews 11.

QUESTIONS FOR DISCUSSION OR REFLECTION

- Jacob blessed his grandsons the same way his father blessed him—with the younger blessed greater than the older. Does this sound logical?

  _____

  _____

  _____

- Do you think Jacob did this for logical, practical reasons? Or does this say something about Jacob's spiritual, God-centered faith?

  _____

  _____

  _____

- Do you think Jacob's many years of difficult living taught him lessons about God's sovereignty?

  _____

  _____

  _____

- What are some lessons Jacob possibly learned? How might these lessons have led him to bless his grandsons the same way he had been blessed by his father?

  _____

  _____

  _____

21 Joseph

—Genesis 37, 39-50; Hebrews 11:22

B‍y faith Joseph, when he was dying, made mention of the departure of the children of Israel, and gave instructions concerning his bones" (Heb. 11:22). If there is one person whose entire life story belongs in Hebrews 11, it is Joseph. And yet, perhaps to make a point, his life story is not mentioned at all.

Joseph was Jacob's favorite son, and as a teenager, he had dreams that gave him a premonition that God would make him rule over his eleven brothers. Partly because of this very dream, his brothers plotted to kill him. But instead, they decided to sell Joseph to traders. The brothers then gave their father false evidence that Joseph had been mauled by wild animals. Jacob believed that his favorite son was dead at age seventeen.

The traders sold Joseph to Potiphar, an officer of Pharaoh in Egypt and captain of the guard. Joseph was very successful as Potiphar's servant, and he eventually became the overseer of everything Potiphar had. Then Potiphar's wife, frustrated that Joseph would not sleep with her, made the false accusation that Joseph had tried to violate her. Joseph was imprisoned.

Even in prison, Joseph was successful. The keeper of the prison trusted Joseph with authority there! His ability to interpret dreams became prominent when he was in prison. Yet, he was forgotten by Pharaoh's chief butler, whose dream Joseph correctly interpreted. Joseph was left in prison an additional two years. When Pharaoh ended up having a dream that no Egyptian could interpret, Pharaoh's chief butler finally remembered Joseph.

Joseph interpreted Pharaoh's dream, and then instructed Pharaoh on what to do. There would be seven good, prosperous years followed by seven years of drought and famine, Joseph told Pharaoh. Joseph then presented a strategy to prepare for the famine, and Pharaoh made Joseph second in command over Egypt!

Joseph's prophecy and strategy for survival were very effective, and Egypt was the only nation in the region that stayed fed during the famine. Joseph's family heard about the food available in Egypt. After dramatic reunion encounters, Joseph's father and brothers moved to Egypt with their households and possessions. And Pharaoh gave Joseph's family prime territory in Egypt, where they prospered. After Jacob died, Joseph's brothers feared that Joseph would retaliate for the evil they inflicted on him when they sold him in the first place. But Joseph responded, "Do not be afraid, for am I in the place of God? But as for you, you meant evil against me; but God meant it for good, in order to bring it about as it is this day, to save many people alive. Now therefore, do not be afraid; I will provide for you and your little ones" (Gen. 50:19-21).

There is so much to learn from Joseph's story. It says so much about faith, perseverance, a positive attitude, inner peace, and forgiveness. But the author of Hebrews has a different emphasis. Hebrews 11:22 simply makes reference to Genesis 50:24-25, when a 110 year old Joseph said to his brothers, "I am dying; but God will surely visit you, and bring you out of this land to the land which He swore to Abraham, to Isaac, and to Jacob. . . .God will surely visit you, and you shall carry my bones up from here."

Joseph's personal story was captivating. Yet, he remembered that what God had accomplished through his life was only a small part of what God had promised to His beloved people. Even as his family was prospering and thriving in Egypt, Joseph remembered that Egypt was not their final destination.

QUESTIONS FOR
DISCUSSION OR REFLECTION

- We have to face many obstacles in life. When you reflect on your life, is your faith in God overshadowed by your ability to endure and prosper in spite of adversity?

  _____

  _____

  _____

- What means more to you on a daily basis: God's promise for your soul's eternal home, or your amazement at how God has helped you conquer adversity in the past?

  _____

  _____

  _____

- What does Hebrews 11:22 tell you about God's priorities in this matter?

  _____

  _____

  _____

22 The Parents of Moses

—Exodus 1:1 - 2:10; Hebrews 11:23

After Joseph died, the people of Israel continued to prosper in Egypt. They grew so strong and powerful that the Egyptian kings began to fear them. And eventually, a king arose in Egypt who had no memory of Joseph and no reason to show any favor to the people of Israel. This Pharaoh afflicted them with hard labor. And yet, the more they were afflicted, the more they multiplied. When Hebrew midwives shrewdly refused to obey orders to kill all Hebrew male babies, Pharaoh ordered that every son born to the Hebrews be thrown into the river to die.

During this time of oppression and hardship, Moses was born. And because Moses was a beautiful child, his parents hid him. "By faith Moses, when he was born, was hidden three months by his parents, because they saw he was a beautiful child; and they were not afraid of the king's command" (Heb. 11:23).

After three months, they could no longer hide him. So instead of just throwing him into the river, they built him a little ark to float him down the river. Moses' aunt watched the ark to see what would become of it. Moses was discovered in the river by Pharaoh's daughter and her servants. She had compassion on the baby, even though she knew he was a Hebrew baby. A Hebrew woman was called to nurse him, and Moses was raised as a son of Pharaoh's daughter. It was she who named him Moses.

QUESTIONS FOR DISCUSSION OR REFLECTION

■ Have you lived through times of affliction or oppression?

_____

_____

_____

■ How were you able to endure such times?

_____

_____

_____

■ What kept you from completely giving up?

_____

_____

_____

■ Moses' parents made special efforts to save him because "he was a beautiful child." Does beauty have the same effect on you?

_____

_____

_____

■ Does beauty remind you of how good and beautiful God is, and embolden you to hope for better things to come?

_____

_____

_____

23 Moses

—Exodus 2:11-14:31; Hebrews 11:24-29

By faith Moses, when he became of age, refused to be called the son of Pharaoh's daughter, choosing rather to suffer affliction with the people of God than to enjoy the passing pleasures of sin, esteeming the reproach of Christ greater than the treasures in Egypt; for he looked to the reward. By faith he forsook Egypt, not fearing the wrath of the king; for he endured as seeing Him who is invisible. By faith he kept the Passover and the sprinkling of blood, lest he who destroyed the firstborn should touch them. By faith they passed through the Red Sea as by dry land, whereas the Egyptians, attempting to do so, were drowned" (Heb. 11:24-29).

Moses was raised in the house of Pharaoh's daughter, and he lived a privileged life as a young person. But his heart's allegiance was with his people, the Hebrews. One day, thinking there were no witnesses, Moses murdered an Egyptian who had beaten a Hebrew. But there were witnesses, and Moses fled from the wrath of Pharaoh. He ended up in the home of a Hebrew priest, and he married one of the priest's daughters.

After a different Pharaoh had taken power, God called on Moses to lead the deliverance of the Hebrew people from Egypt to the Promised Land. And when Moses confronted Pharaoh, the first result was a drastic increase in oppression against the Hebrews by Egyptian taskmasters. God wanted to make it evident that it was through His strength that Israel would be delivered from Egypt. Tactful human negotiations or human force would lead Israel nowhere. Israel's deliverance would occur by means of God's miraculous wonders.

Moses was God's mouthpiece to Pharaoh, and Pharaoh's hardened heart led God to heap many miraculous plagues upon Egypt. But nothing short of a horrendous miraculous massacre would cause Pharaoh to relent. At midnight on a certain night, every firstborn in Egypt died. But every Hebrew lived, because God saw the blood that was sprinkled on the Hebrews' doorposts and passed over their houses without letting the destroyer cause harm. This was the Passover.

God's next miracle was the departure of the people of Israel through the Red Sea, which had parted and dried due to a miraculous wind. Even though the Egyptian army was nearby, the Egyptians were miraculously in total darkness of night, while the Hebrews miraculously had light to see their way across the sea, with walls of water at each side of them. When the natural light of morning came, the Egyptian army gave chase through the sea, but was annihilated by the walls of water that crashed down on them. "So the LORD saved Israel that day out of the hand of the Egyptians, and Israel saw the Egyptians dead on the seashore" (Gen. 14:30).

QUESTIONS FOR DISCUSSION OR REFLECTION

- As a young person, Moses decided that he would rather live for God's eternal promises than for his own pleasure in Pharaoh's family. Are you the same way? Would you rather live for God's eternal promises than for your own pleasure?

  _____

  _____

  _____

- Moses looked forward to the same "reward" (Heb. 11:26) that Enoch had looked forward to centuries earlier (Heb. 11:6). He looked forward to eternal life. He looked forward to Christ. This faith in God's eternal promises preceded God's miracles in Moses' life. Do your eyes look toward eternity?

  _____

  _____

  _____

- Do you look back at what Christ did with the same appreciation that Moses had when looking forward to it?

  _____

  _____

  _____

24 Joshua and Israel's Army at Jericho

—Joshua 3:1-6:21; Hebrews 11:30

By faith the walls of Jericho fell down after they were encircled for seven days" (Heb. 11:30). After Moses died, it was Joshua's responsibility to lead Israel into the Promised Land. His first step was to cross the Jordan River and conquer the walled city of Jericho. All the people groups in the area were already wary of Israel's size, strength, and past success. Israel was powerful enough to conquer these lands by their own human strength. But this was not how God wanted them to do it, and Joshua let God lead God's way.

First, God miraculously caused the overflowing Jordan River to "wall up" upstream to make way for Israel to cross the river on dry land. Then He had the men of Israel's army get circumcised and wait a few days to heal. Then came the "strategy" to conquer the walled city of Jericho, which was completely shut down with no one entering or exiting.

For six days, Israel's army marched around Jericho once a day. Then on the seventh day, they marched around the city seven times. Then they shouted and blew trumpets, and the wall of the city just fell down flat. Israel's army then marched in and annihilated Jericho.

God's miracles were just as astounding when Israel entered the Promised Land as they were when Israel left Egypt forty years earlier. When God does things His miraculous way, it is obvious.

QUESTIONS FOR
DISCUSSION OR REFLECTION

■ Even though God's miracles are obvious, churches often attempt to duplicate God's miracles by creating certain worshipful moods. Can you tell the difference between when God performs a miracle in your heart and when worshipful moods give your heart a non-miraculous emotional experience?

_____

_____

_____

■ Do you anticipate that God will perform miracles in your life, or do you try to control your own circumstances?

_____

_____

_____

25 Rahab

—Joshua 2:1-24, 6:22-25; Hebrews 11:31

Before Joshua and Israel's army miraculously crossed the Jordan River on dry land, two spies were sent to examine the whole area, and especially the walled city of Jericho. At Jericho, perhaps to make themselves inconspicuous, the spies stayed in the house of a harlot named Rahab. Her house was at the wall of the city. But word of the spies got to Jericho's king, and he sent pursuers to Rahab's house. Rahab hid the spies and lied to the men sent from the king. She also instructed the spies on the best way to escape. "By faith the harlot Rahab did not perish with those who did not believe, when she received the spies with peace" (Heb. 11:31). In return for her efforts, Rahab wanted herself and her family to be spared when Israel overthrew her city.

Rahab believed that Israel's God was the true God because of the miracles that happened in Israel's exodus from Egypt and in their more recent conquests. The people in her city were terrified that the Hebrews were so close to them, and Rahab was convinced that Israel would conquer Jericho. Her convictions emboldened her to side with the spies and ask that Israel protect those in her house. Her wish was granted, and Israel made sure that all those in Rahab's house were kept safe while the rest of the city was destroyed.

QUESTIONS FOR
DISCUSSION REFLECTION

- Rahab did not believe she deserved to be rescued by Israel. Rather, she deeply believed that her only hope was that Israel would protect her. God honored her faith. If you are a Christian, your undeserved salvation is through Israel, because Jesus Christ came through Israel. How bold is your faith in God?

  _____

  _____

  _____

- Are you willing to take the same risks Rahab took?

  _____

  _____

- Will you risk punishment in this life in order to pursue the eternal blessings that God can give through Jesus Christ?

  _____

  _____

26 Too Many to Mention

—Isaiah 9:6; Hebrews 11:32-40

And what more shall I say? For the time would fail me to tell of Gideon and Barak and Samson and Jephthah, also of David and Samuel and the prophets: who through faith subdued kingdoms, worked righteousness, obtained promises, stopped the mouths of lions, quenched the violence of fire, escaped the edge of the sword, out of weakness were made strong, became valiant in battle, turned to fight the armies of the aliens. Women received their dead raised to life again. Others were tortured, not accepting deliverance, that they might obtain a better resurrection. Still others had trial of mockings and scourgings, yes, and of chains and imprisonment. They were stoned, they were sawn in two, were tempted, were slain with the sword. They wandered about in sheepskins and goatskins, being destitute, afflicted, tormented—of whom the world was not worthy. They wandered in deserts and mountains, in dens and caves of the earth. And all these, having obtained a good testimony through faith, did not receive the promise, God having provided something better for us, that they should not be made perfect apart from us" (Heb. 11:32-40).

Faith does not necessarily lead to success or happy endings in this life. But since all these people who had faith in God placed their faith in God's promises for eternal life, there is no need to separate the "success stories" from the "tragedies." They are all success stories in God's eyes.

One glaringly tragic success story of faith in action is represented by the phrase ". . . were sawn in two" (Heb. 11:37). Though the Bible does not mention any particular person being sawn in two, Jewish sources outside the Bible indicate that this happened to the prophet Isaiah. Isaiah had a horrific death, but his faith in God was solid. In Isaiah 9:6, he wrote the following prophesy more than 700 years before it was fulfilled by Jesus:

> For unto us a Child is born,
> Unto us a Son is given;
> And the government will be upon His shoulder.
> And His name will be called
> Wonderful, Counselor, Mighty God,
> Everlasting Father, Prince of Peace.

Notice how he writes, "a Child is born" and then "a Son is given." The shift from "born" to "given" tells a lot about exactly where Isaiah placed his faith: in the coming Messiah, Jesus Christ. Though He became a child 2,000 years ago, Jesus was God's "Son" from eternity past. If Jesus was neither our Creator nor the Son of God from eternity past, then He could not be Israel's Messiah, and all of these "Stories of Faith" are random. Thankfully, all those mentioned in Hebrews 11 placed their faith in the same unseen thing that they each hoped for, namely that God's perfect sacrifice would redeem them to righteousness in God's eyes and restore them to eternal life.

Faith often seems like an abstract concept. However, once we see that every story of faith in Hebrews 11 points to the same unseen thing hoped for, the first two verses of Hebrews 11 become much more palpable: "Now faith is the substance of things hoped for, the evidence of things not seen. For by it the elders obtained a good testimony."

QUESTIONS FOR
DISCUSSION OR REFLECTION

■ Does faith still seem like an abstract concept to you? Or does it sound like a solid concept that has stayed consistent from the beginning of time?

_____

_____

_____

■ Is your faith strong like the faith of the men and women mentioned in Hebrews 11? If not, why not?

_____

_____

_____

27 Jesus, Peter, and a Deceptive Fig Tree

—Mark 11:12-26

During the peak of Jesus' earthly ministry, He examined a fig tree that had leaves earlier than it should have. Fruit usually grows along with leaves on fig trees, but Jesus found no fruit on this one. So Jesus told the tree, "Let no one eat from you ever again" (Mark 11:14). Jesus then proceeded to Jerusalem, where He drove out traders and money changers from the temple. The specific problem Jesus had with them is revealed in Mark 11:17, where He taught, "Is it not written, 'My house shall be called a house of prayer for all nations'? But you have made it a den of thieves."

All of the busy activities inside the temple made temple life look deceptively healthy, like the fig tree with all the leaves. But when He inspected more closely, Jesus found that the temple was no longer a house of prayer and that the fig tree had no fruit.

The next morning, Jesus and His twelve closest followers passed by the fig tree again, and it was completely dried up. Peter remembered what Jesus told the tree the day before, and he said to Jesus, "Rabbi, look! The fig tree which You cursed has withered away" (Mark 11:21). Jesus' first words of response were, "Have faith in God."

Peter and the rest of the apostles would later be commissioned by the resurrected Jesus to spread the good news about Jesus all over the world. This led to the existence of churches all around the world. In preparation for this worldwide church, Jesus made sure He gave His apostles memorable, graphic images of what He hated. Jesus hated houses of worship that looked prosperous, but upon close inspection were fruitless. Jesus wants fruit, not deceptive outward signs of fruit.

What is this "fruit" that Jesus wants to see? He answers this question in Mark 11:22-26, where He emphasizes that we are to "have faith in God" (as opposed to people or programs). This faith is to contain no doubt at all. Also, it is to be free of pain. We are to forgive those who hurt us, so that we may receive God's forgiveness.

When we hold on to our pain and refuse to forgive, the result is a self-protective wall that severely limits our faith. Forgive the ones who hurt you, and forget your pain. Then you will be able to put your faith in God.

QUESTIONS FOR
DISCUSSION OR REFLECTION

- Do you go to a church where you can look spiritually healthy by wearing the "fig leaves" of a big smile and an active lifestyle?

  _____

  _____

  _____

- Similarly, do you go to a church where you can look spiritually healthy by wearing the "fig leaves" of a serious, pious demeanor and a mundane life? In either case, inspect yourself as closely as God sees you. Is there fruit? Is there faith in God?

  _____

  _____

  _____

- Are pain and unforgiveness blocking you from having faith in God?

  _____

  _____

  _____

28 Scripture

—2 Samuel 23:1-3; Isaiah 59:21;
Jeremiah 1:9; 2 Timothy 3:16; 2 Peter 1:21

What do you think the Bible is? How accurate is it? Is it really God's Word? Your answers to these questions reveal a lot about your heart, soul, and mind. If you think the Bible is not completely accurate and not entirely God's Word, then you are left in a difficult position. You care about God and want to believe in Him, but you don't completely trust the only book that compiles His Word. How deep can such faith be?

The Bible says that "All Scripture is given by inspiration of God" (2 Tim. 3:16). This means that every individual Scripture, or book within the Bible, is inspired by God. The Bible as a whole was completely assembled by scholars around 400 A.D. But each individual Scripture (book of the Bible) was written exactly as God wanted it, over the course of about 1,500 years. Even while granting each human writer the use of his own personal literary style and intellect, God was able to oversee and inspire each Scripture as it was written in its original language.

We in the English-speaking world have many Bible translations to choose from. There is no such thing as a perfect English translation. Sometimes certain shades of meaning will inevitably get lost in translation. However, some translations are very accurate, and others are not. In this book, every Scripture quotation is taken from the same very accurate English translation, The New King James Version. This translation does what any accurate translation does: it takes each Scripture in its original language, and expresses an accurate English equivalent for every word, phrase, and sentence.

Many other Bible translations sacrifice precise meaning in order to make it easier for today's readers to enjoy. There are even some popular paraphrases of the Bible. The authors of paraphrases do not necessarily consider the meaning of the Scriptures in their original languages. They often just reword or rethink other English translations. The result is an easy to read book that looks like a Bible but is not. Paraphrases should not be granted authority as though they were the Bible itself, because they change more than just the Bible's vocabulary. They change the Bible's meaning.

QUESTIONS FOR DISCUSSION OR REFLECTION

■ Does the accuracy of your Bible's translation matter to you?

_____

_____

_____

■ When you read your Bible, do you revere and respect it as God's Word?

_____

_____

_____

Conclusion

The intent of this book, stated in the introduction, is to reveal various "Obstacles to Faith" that cause our soil to seem stony, thorny, or "poor like the wayside," and to tell many "Stories of Faith" that clarify what good soil is like. These soils are what Jesus spoke about in His parable of the sower and the seeds.

When Jesus talked about the kingdom of heaven in this parable, He was not just talking about what life would be like after Jesus' ministry. He was describing how the kingdom of heaven already was.

Christians who lose faith because of the concerns of this life are similar to the people of Israel after they crossed through the parted waters of the Red Sea. These Hebrew people often lacked faith that God would provide for them.

They had seen God's miracles. God's miracles changed their lives. Yet when the miracles were no longer visible, they quickly forgot how faithful God is.

We Christians do the same thing. When we received Jesus as Savior, we benefited from God's greatest miracle just like one of Joshua's soldiers who benefited from God's miracle and crossed the Jordan River on dry ground. It was an astonishing miracle. Yet, just like the people of Israel after they entered the Promised Land, we forget how faithful God is. Our soil keeps getting stony or thorny.

Israel is God's chosen people. Yet, God chose to bless the whole world through Jesus Christ, Israel's Messiah. This was not a random act. Jesus was intimately involved throughout all of history before and after He walked the earth 2,000 years ago.

Our faith in God is similar to Rahab's faith. Rahab, a non-Hebrew, knew about God's past miracles on behalf of Israel, and she believed that Israel's God was the true God. She knew that her only hope was to take refuge in the God of Israel for salvation. This resulted in both King David and Jesus Christ being among Rahab's descendants. She believed in God's eternal promises, and God honored her faith by delivering His eternal promises through her line of descendants.

We have learned of God's greatest miracle, forgiveness of sins through God's only Son, Jesus Christ. And, if we have taken refuge in Him, we are now descendants of God's righteousness, just like Abraham, Rahab, David, and so many others. Jesus affirmed this concept in a conversation with the Pharisees recorded in Matthew 22:41-45:

While the Pharisees were gathered together, Jesus asked them, saying, "What do you think about the Christ? Whose Son is He?" They said to Him, "The Son of David." He said to them, "How then does David in the Spirit call Him 'Lord,' saying: 'The LORD said to my Lord, sit at My right hand, till I make Your enemies Your footstool'? If David then calls Him 'Lord,' how is He his Son?"

Here in Matthew 22, Jesus is quoting what David wrote in Psalms 110:1. Isaiah also wrote about this complicated, yet deeply meaningful truth. Salvation was to arrive through God's Son, and God's Son was with God from eternity past. Neither God nor his Son nor His Holy Spirit were created. They are the One true God, the Trinity. Yet Christ would be born as a Child, become a Man, and shed His blood to pay the penalty for our sins—to redeem us.

Does this sound overwhelming? Is this too complicated for you to understand or even want to understand? As intimidating as these ideas may sound, if you have received Jesus Christ as your Savior, you have nothing to be afraid of. To the contrary, you have God's promises for eternal life to comfort and strengthen you. "For you were once darkness, but now you are light in the Lord. Walk as children of light" (Eph. 5:8).

To order additional copies of

TOUGH
LIFE
LESSONS

Have your credit card ready and call

Toll free: (877) 421-READ (7323)

or order online at: www.winepressbooks.com

To contact the author, write to:

Andrew Kalitka
PO Box 5393
Magnolia, MA 01930
www.toughlifelessons.net